Cultural Celebrations

An Imprint of Pop!
popbooksonline.com

DIWALI

by Elizabeth Andrews

WELCOME TO DiscoverRoo!

This book is filled with videos, puzzles, games, and more! Scan the QR codes* while you read, or visit the website below to make this book pop.

popbooksonline.com/diwali

abdobooks.com

Published by Pop!, a division of ABDO, PO Box 398166, Minneapolis, Minnesota 55439.

Printed in the United States of America, North Mankato, Minnesota.

102023
012024

Cover Photo: Shutterstock Images
Interior Photos: Getty Images, Shutterstock Images, Wikimedia Commons
Editor: Emily Dreher
Series Designer: Colleen McLaren

Library of Congress Control Number: 2023938821

Publisher's Cataloging-in-Publication Data

Names: Andrews, Elizabeth, author.
Title: Diwali / by Elizabeth Andrews
Description: Minneapolis, Minnesota : Pop!, 2024 | Series: Cultural celebrations | Includes online resources and index
Identifiers: ISBN 9781098245351 (lib. bdg.) | ISBN 9781098245917 (ebook)
Subjects: LCSH: Diwali--Juvenile literature. | Divali--Juvenile literature. | Fasts and feasts--Hinduism--Juvenile literature. | Holidays--Juvenile literature. | Cultural sociology--Juvenile literature.
Classification: DDC 394.26--dc23

*Scanning QR codes requires a web-enabled smart device with a QR code reader app and a camera.

TABLE OF CONTENTS

CHAPTER 1

LIGHTS AND COLOR

Ravi's house is full of color and lights. He's spent the past two days cleaning and decorating with his family. It's finally time to celebrate by lighting the clay oil lamps called *diyas* and going out to watch fireworks. It is Diwali!

WATCH A VIDEO HERE!

Boys often wear new long shirts called kurtas for Diwali.

The dot women and girls wear on their forehead is called a bindi.

Ravi and his family are all dressed nicely. Before the fireworks, they say their prayers to the goddess Lakshmi.

They place flowers by her statue and light the diyas. After their prayer is done, they all go to town. During the fireworks show, Ravi gets to eat a yummy treat from a food stand.

Flowers are sometimes hung on strings for decoration or laid in patterns on the ground.

Diyas are oil lamps made from clay. They are lit to rid homes of evil.

Diwali is also known as the **Festival of Lights**. It is a major religious holiday for Hindus. Diwali lasts five days. Each day has its own special traditions to follow.

DID YOU KNOW?

Diwali is also known as Deepavali, Dipavali, Dewali, Deepawali, or the Festival of Lights.

Diwali began in India but has become one of the most widely celebrated holidays around the world.

CHAPTER 2

HISTORY OF DIWALI

Diwali started as a Hindu holiday. Hinduism is the oldest religion still practiced today. There are several versions of the Diwali story. All stories **honor** the **triumph** of good over evil. The stories of Diwali follow the god Vishnu. Vishnu oversees keeping the **universe** safe.

LEARN MORE HERE!

Some Hindus believe there are 330 million gods and goddesses.

After saving Sita, Rama returned to his home after 14 years of unfair exile.

Vishnu interacts with humans in different forms throughout Hindu history. Sometimes he comes to earth as a lesser god or human royalty. A popular Diwali story **features** Vishnu as the god Rama. Prince Rama saved his wife, Sita, from an evil king. Sita was a form of the goddess Lakshmi.

Forms of Vishnu are often blue to represent his connection to the sky.

Krishna is believed to be the eighth form of Vishnu. Krishna is considered a Hindu god.

Another version of the Diwali story follows Lord Krishna, a different form of Vishnu. Krishna defeats an evil king who had **imprisoned** 16,000 women. Again, good defeats evil in that story. Like Prince Rama, Lord Krishna is married to a form of the goddess Lakshmi. Queen Rukmini is his wife.

Lakshmi is the Hindu goddess most closely tied to Diwali. She is the goddess of wealth, good fortune, luck, youth, and beauty. She is Vishnu's wife. During Diwali, her **worshippers** ask for her blessings in the new year.

Lakshmi was born on a lotus flower.

CHAPTER 3

THE FIVE DAYS OF DIWALI

Diwali leads up to the Hindu New Year. On the first day of Diwali, people clean their homes. Making a home clean and bright invites positivity. People also buy metal items, new cars, and jewelry on the first day of Diwali. They bake sweets and pray to Lakshmi for good fortune.

EXPLORE LINKS HERE!

Turmeric, cumin, and cardamom are spices often used in Indian food.

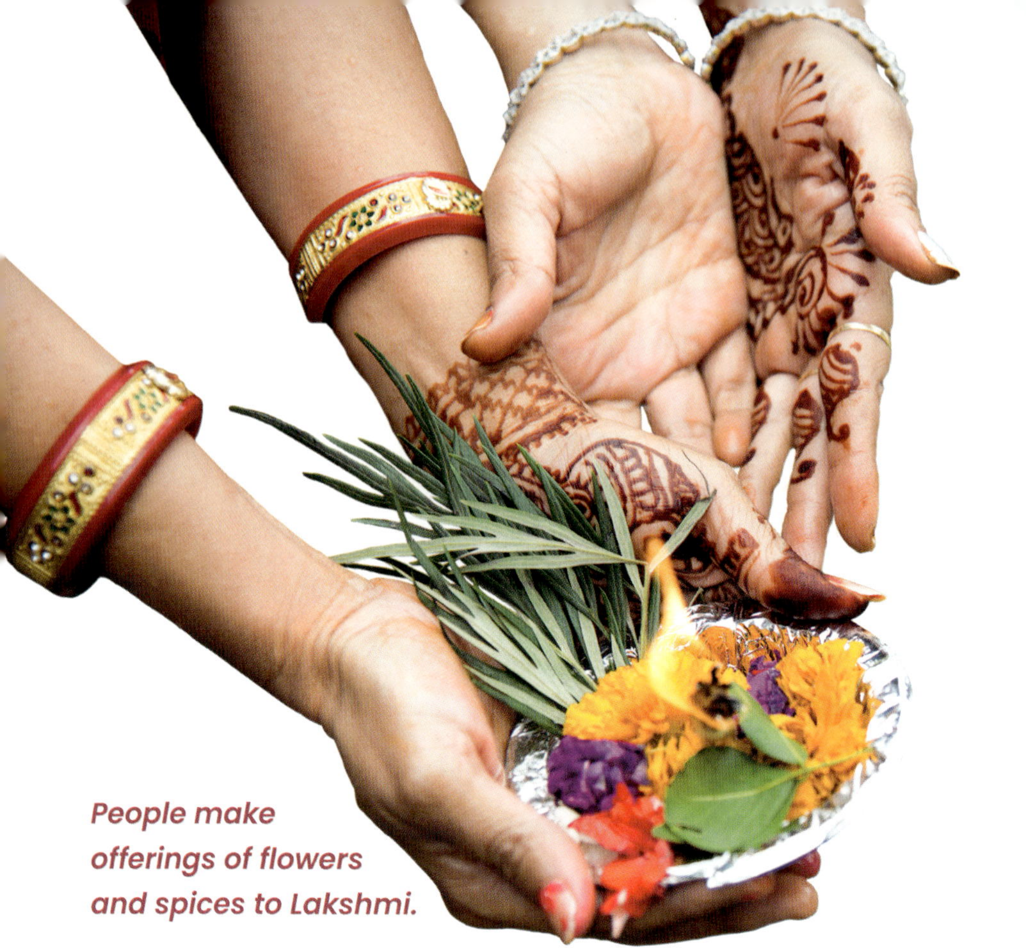

People make offerings of flowers and spices to Lakshmi.

On the second day of Diwali, it's time to decorate! Diwali is the **Festival** of Lights, so people dress their homes

DID YOU KNOW?

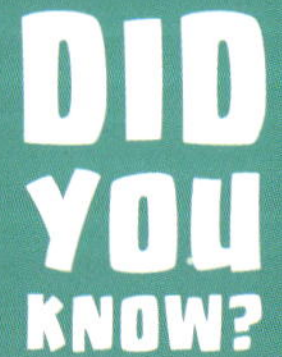

Hindus pray for the **souls** of their **ancestors** on the second day of Diwali.

with diyas, *rangoli*, lanterns, marigold flowers, and string lights. Diyas are made specifically for Diwali. Rangoli are beautiful floor artworks. The clean home and decorations are supposed to be inviting for Lakshmi's visit.

Rangoli are made with colored sand and flowers.

Day three of Diwali is the main event. It's called Diwali Day. Families and friends may have a puja for Lakshmi. Puja is a Hindu prayer ceremony. People may visit a temple. Families gather to light their diyas and exchange gifts. The goddess Lakshmi enters decorated homes to bless people with good fortune for the new year.

Offerings are given during puja. They are gifts to honor and thank Lakshmi.

Diwali treats include milk cakes, **gulab jamun,** *and* **jalebi.**

On day three, people in India and all over the world eat delicious food such as puri with a curry or dal, crispy samosas, *aloo bonda*, and of course, more sweets! The third day of Diwali is the last day of the year. People reflect on the good and bad of the past year. Day three is also when big street festivals are held.

FIVE DAYS OF DIWALI

Clean the home. Shop for gifts and decorations.

DAY TWO

Decorate the home. Create rangoli.

Day four of Diwali is the first day of the new year. Friends and families gather again to eat and wish each other good health and **prosperity**.

They exchange gifts. The fifth day of Diwali is a day to **honor** siblings. Sisters often make sweets for their brothers.

CHAPTER 4

ALL AROUND THE WORLD

Diwali is celebrated by one billion people around the world. This means that there are many ways and places for people to take part in the **Festival** of Lights.

COMPLETE AN ACTIVITY HERE!

Jalebi are spiral-shaped fried sweets. They are juicy on the inside.

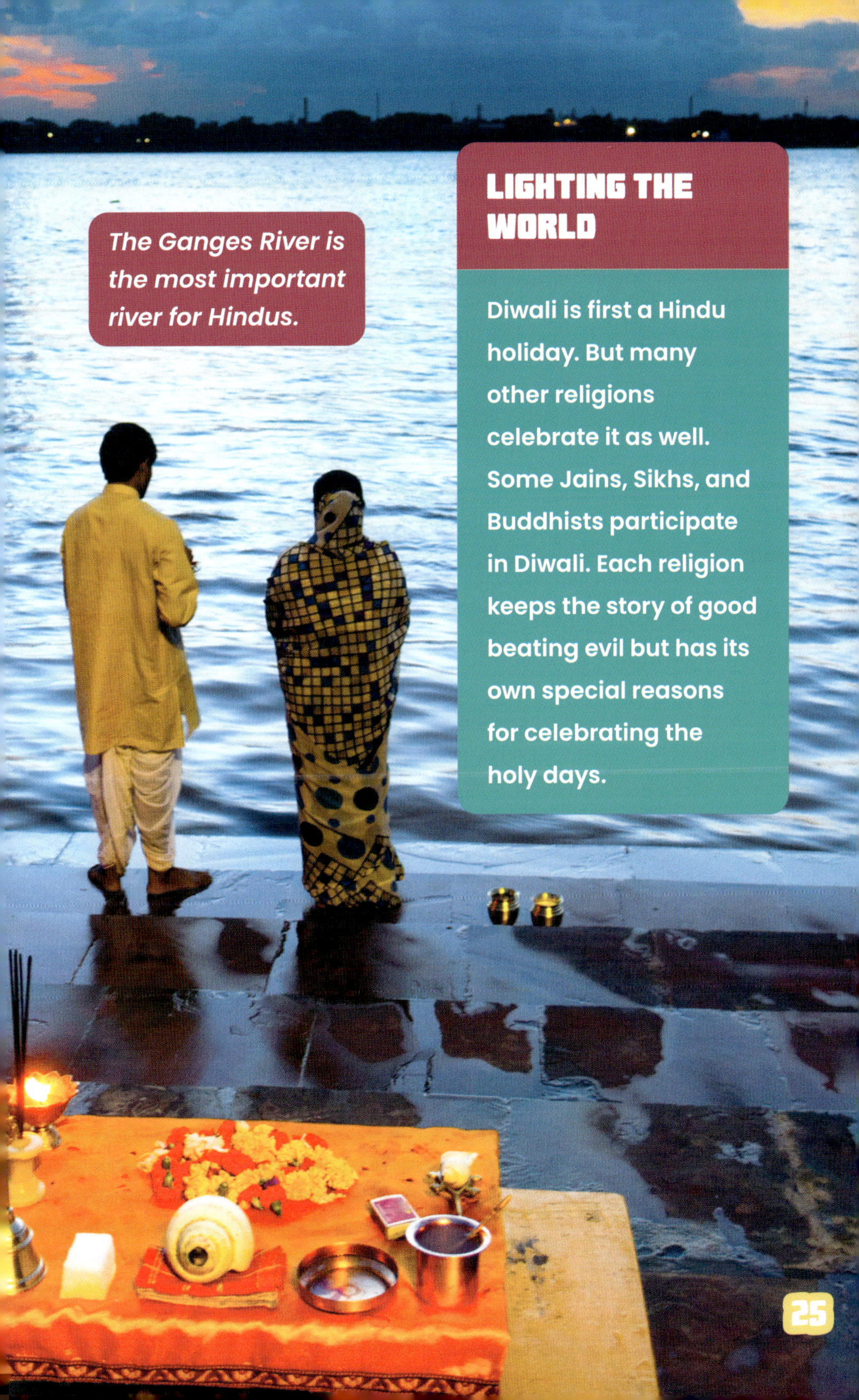

The Ganges River is the most important river for Hindus.

LIGHTING THE WORLD

Diwali is first a Hindu holiday. But many other religions celebrate it as well. Some Jains, Sikhs, and Buddhists participate in Diwali. Each religion keeps the story of good beating evil but has its own special reasons for celebrating the holy days.

Cities in India are very busy. Even more people visit during Diwali.

India has the largest population of any country. Diwali is its most important holiday. All around the country fun events take place. Varanasi, India, hosts large markets where people can shop for jewelry and decorations. Then on Diwali Day, they stop along the Ganges River and see fireworks displays.

In Mumbai, India, children make their own lanterns. Families and friends take walks along roads lined with lanterns and lights. They can get sweet treats from street stalls. Ayodhya, India, is the city that Prince Rama returned to after exile. The people of Ayodhya light millions of diyas along the Ghaghara River.

Giant paper lanterns decorate the outside of a Hindu temple.

Many people in the United Kingdom celebrate Diwali. London and Leicester, England, host events. There's traditional dancing, music, and markets. Leicester has one of the largest Diwali celebrations outside of India. City streets are lit up to create the "Golden Mile." And on Diwali Day, there is a large fireworks display.

Fireworks may be used less in future Diwali celebrations to protect the environment.

The streets of Little India, Singapore, are alight for Diwali.

Diwali celebrates good overcoming evil. It is a holiday full of hope, light, and color! People around the world invite positivity and hope into the new year.

MAKING CONNECTIONS

TEXT-TO-SELF

What part of the Diwali celebration were you most interested in? Please explain your answer.

TEXT-TO-TEXT

Have you read any books about other Hindu holidays? If so, what did that holiday have in common with Diwali?

TEXT-TO-WORLD

Why do you think Diwali is so widely celebrated? If you were to celebrate Diwali, where in the world would you like to go?

GLOSSARY

ancestor — a family member from an earlier time.

feature — to play an important part.

festival — a time of celebration marked by special events.

honor — to regard with great respect.

imprison — to put someone or something in prison.

prosperity — success or wealth.

soul — a nonmaterial part of a living being.

triumph — the winning of a great victory or success.

universe — all existing things, including the Earth and heavens.

worshipper — a person who honors a god or goddess by praying or through other acts.

INDEX

DiscoverRoo!

ONLINE RESOURCES

This book is filled with videos, puzzles, games, and more! Scan the QR codes* while you read, or visit the website below to make this book pop.

popbooksonline.com/diwali

*Scanning QR codes requires a web-enabled smart device with a QR code reader app and a camera.